DEER STORY 2

About the Author
Raised in Willowick, Ohio, a small suburb of Cleveland. I was an Empath before even knowing what that was. I had an extremely abusive mother who scared all the neighborhood kids away with her constant yelling but I also had wonderful, supportive, loving Dad who was my best Friend.

The Very Most Incredible. Spectacular. Miraculous. Amazing

DEER STORY

You'll Ever Read In Your Life

By Catherine Mathews Moore

DEER STORY

BY CATHERINE MATHEWS MOORE

The Very Most Incredible, Spectacular, Miraculous, Amazing

You'll Ever Read In Your Life And it's All True

XULON PRESS

Xulon Press
2301 Lucien Way #415
Maitland, FL 32751
407.339.4217
www.xulonpress.com

Printed in the United States of America.

ISBN-13: 978-1-6305-0419-9

I dedicate this book to my children, my grandchildren, and those to come; to my beloved hubby Bud Moore; and my Dad

Warren Kenneth Mathews, WWII Honoree.

My youngest Son Danny, a baby deer just came up to him and wouldn't stop licking his hands.

I lived on a **265-acre farm in Ohio. It was a beau**
tiful, wonderful Farm to live on. It was a dairy farm
with an enormous barn. I loved to go up in the barn's
hayloft to listen to the rain on the tin roof when it
was raining, enjoy the sweet smell of hay, and listen
to the barn swallows.

There was a wonderful **200**-year-old brick house that was once used as a schoolhouse. It was a nine-room house with a full basement and attic. The kitchen was added on without the basement, so in the winter, the kitchen was almost as cold as it was outside, and we'd have to dress warm to go in there. But, it was enormous and had one of those great, big, old-fashioned sinks that was big enough to give your toddler a bath in.

The house had a covered porch that wrapped around nearly three sides of the house. In the attic, you could see through the bricks where the mortar had crumbled away, and we had a huge coal and wood-burning furnace.

The rooms were all big, except for the baby's room right off the master bedroom and the library. I loved everything about that farm. It was a great blessing and gift from God that I was forever thankful for and a wonderful place to raise a family.

On my way home from Cleveland one night, in the wee hours of the morning, a deer jumped out of the field right in front of me! It happened so fast; I barely had time to respond, but there it was. And, **WHAT !!??** It had a baby with it!

As I quickly veered to my left to avoid them, out popped another baby deer, and to my shock and horror, I hit it!

I had always loved deer, and I prayed my Heart out that Jesus would make him ok. I was shaking and crying and praying! With the deer in my arms, I rushed to the door, then kicked it, screaming for someone to let me in.

My husband opened the door, then quickly slammed it shut while yelling at me, "You're not bringing that in here."

"Bet me." I yelled back as I kicked the door open and laid the fawn down on the kitchen floor, "Get me a blanket!"

Though I got my way, my husband wasn't giving up yet as he kept yelling at me about the many dangers of bringing a deer in the house. "What do you think is going to happen when it comes too? It'll be kicking and breaking everything in the house, including you. It'll be bouncing off the walls, bringing its ticks and other bugs and diseases in here. Get it back outside!"

I knew he had a good point, so I took it back out-side and as I did, it began waking up. It kicked itself right out of my arms and started running all over the place, including right back out into the street with that rush hour traffic. Then, it instinctively tried to cross the bridge to return to its family. I couldn't let it try to do that for fear that it would surely be killed, so I had to block its path until it finally gave up, and I was able to steer it into the field in back of my house where I knew there was another herd of deer that just might hopefully accept it.

I often sat on the picnic table in my back yard in the hopes that I would catch a glimpse of "my deer" with the herd back there.

Ok, that's not me!

I was hoping to see "**My Deer**" when the herd came up from the lake and the pine forest for the salt lick that we always put out for them. They had been doing that for several years, so we kept leaving it out for them. We could often see them from my kitchen window.

The rest of the summer passed without any sign of my deer. I called him "my deer" because I never could decide on a name for it, and my husband warned me against doing so. The reason being that if it was found dead, supposedly, it won't hurt as bad.

Then just as summer began turning into, autumn there it was.

It was alive!

Not that!

That's Frankenstein, you big goof! Yes, my beautiful deer was alive. I could tell it was the deer I hit because of the scar above it's right eye.

It made me sad that I had scared it for life, but it was alive and looking really good. I noticed that it wasn't exactly "with" the herd, but it was close to them. I guessed they just hadn't completely accepted it yet, but they hadn't chased it away either, so there was still hope.

My husband had also warned me against naming the two baby squirrels that I raised the summer before that had fallen out of trees during a bad storm. One was a flying squirrel only a few days old, and the other was a fox squirrel.

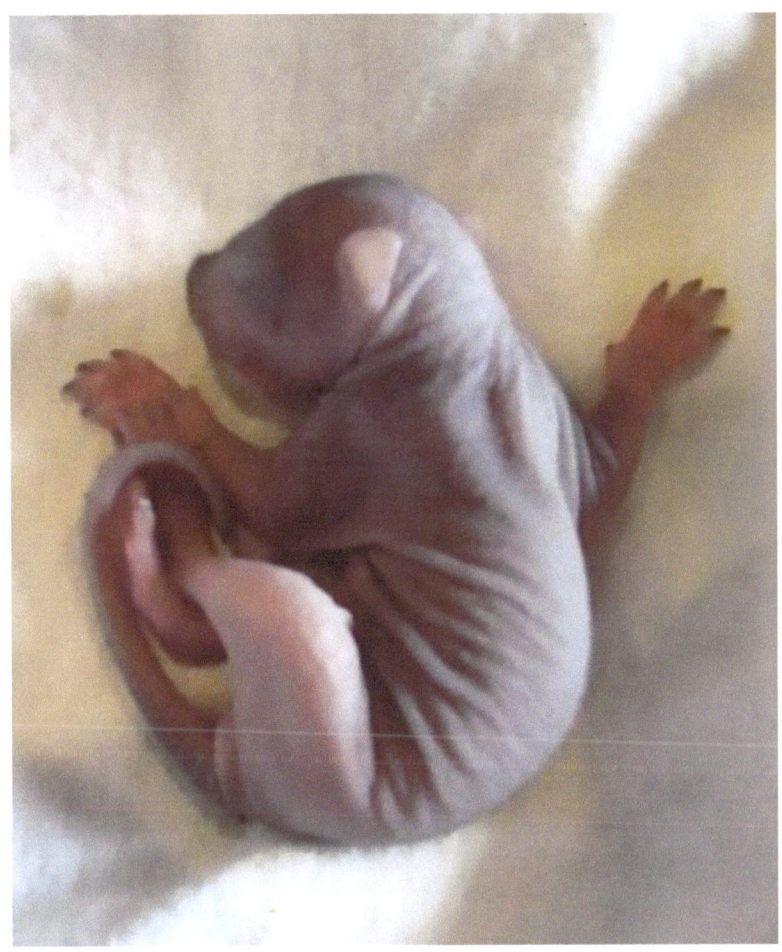

We didn't know what they were at the time because they were so tiny and looked more like mice, but I fed them with an eyedropper until they could eat stale bread soaked in the milk formula I made myself out of distilled water, **Carnation Evaporated Milk**, a little sugar syrup, and one raw egg yolk. Later, they grew into what they really were and what a joy they were then.

They would wake me up chattering and squawking, and the bigger they got, the more they squawked and ran their tiny little toes (and sharp claws) all over me and even in my hair. I couldn't fix their breakfast fast enough for them, but they were so much fun.

The flying squirrel would leap from the top of the curtains, heading right at my face, and if I wasn't paying attention, it would do just that, land on my face and dig it's claws into me.

Since I had raised them both together the, fox squirrel thought it could do that too. But, one leap proved to him that he wasn't up to the challenge, as he went splat, landing flat on his face on the hardwood floor. Yikes!

When they got big enough, I had to let them go, so they could learn to survive as wild squirrels. That was a sad day, and I really missed them even if I hadn't named them. But a few times when I was laying out in the backyard sunning myself, they would pop out of the pine tree next to me and run down the entire length of my body from my head to my feet just like they did so many times before I let them go.

The first time they did that I thought, I was being attacked by rabid aliens! But, I quickly realized it was them, just like **Pixie** and **Dixie**, and it was so cool to see they had remained together.

Ok, those aren't aliens.

They're ducks!

Can't you tell a duck from an alien?

Now behind our house was a field, a pine forest, a lake, and a little creek that I used to go down to in the summer to sleep by when it was too hot. We didn't have air conditioning, and I'd throw my sleeping bag down next to it, and I would drift into a deep and peaceful sleep, just listening to the babbling brook.

Then one morning down by the creek, I felt some-thing leaning against my back. Knowing that nobody knew about my "sacred spot," I opened my eyes to see a deer hoof like just six inches from my nose. I dared not move so as not to startle it for fear it might bolt and take my nose with it. I was real still, and I could hear it slurping the water from the creek. Soon, I could hear others slurping in the creek.

As it finished drinking, it slowly walked across the creek, and as it did I saw behind it, not fifty feet away was the great, great grandpappy of them all with antlers the size of oak trees, just watching me. As we locked eyes, it was as if he was reading my very soul and saying with a twinkle in his eye, "I know exactly how much you're enjoying this."

As the deer with its back up against mine stretched and pushed against me, I began to hear others around me drinking from the creek and slowly crossing it to wander off with the last baby deer with its back against my back and left. I waited still until I could barely hear them before getting up, and to my surprise and great joy, I saw all around me where the deer had slept and matted down the tall grass.

Naturally, I praised God. This herd had slept with me the entire night. That was unheard of. Nothing like this was even possible! I pondered this amazing situation, trying to make some sense out of it with zillions of questions racing threw my brain.

As I folded my sleeping bag and gathered the few things I had brought down there with me, I was suddenly startled by a stomp on the ground. I jumped. As I turned around, there it was again. The great, great grandpappy of them all was back and just looking at me, but this time not more than seven feet away. Then what? As my eyes focused better and I shook off the sleep, there it was.

Could it be? There was that scar above his right eye! It was "me deer"! My deer that I had struck with my van several years ago. My deer! I collapsed to my knees. What an amazing surprise. What an amazingly, wonderful blessing. I thank You and praise You, Lord Jesus.

THE END